PRESIDENTS

LYNDON B. JOHNSON

A MyReportLinks.com Book

Randy Schultz

MyReportLinks.com Books

an imprint of

 Enslow Publishers, Inc. E

Box 398, 40 Industrial Road
Berkeley Heights, NJ 07922
USA

MyReportLinks.com Books, an imprint of Enslow Publishers, Inc.

Library of Congress Cataloging-in-Publication Data

Schultz, Randy.
 Lyndon B. Johnson / Randy Schultz.
  p. cm. — (Presidents)
 Includes bibliographical references (p.) and index.
 Summary: Explores the life of our nation's thirty-sixth
president, whose administration became known for his
"Great Society" politics and its involvement in the Vietnam War.
  ISBN 0-7660-5011-4
  1. Johnson. Lyndon B. (Lyndon Baines), 1908–1973—Juvenile
literature. 2. Presidents–United States–Biography—Juvenile literature.
 [1. Johnson, Lyndon B. (Lyndon Baines), 1908–1973. 2. Presidents.] I. Title. II. Series.
 E847 .S36 2002
 973.923'092—dc2l
 [B]
            2001006847

Printed in the United States of America

10 9 8 7 6 5 4 3 2 1

To Our Readers:
Through the purchase of this book, you and your library gain access to the Report Links that specifically back up this book.
The Publisher will provide access to the Report Links that back up this book and will keep these Report Links up to date on **www.myreportlinks.com** for three years from the book's first publication date.
We have done our best to make sure all Internet addresses in this book were active and appropriate when we went to press. However, the author and the Publisher have no control over, and assume no liability for, the material available on those Internet sites or on other Web sites they may link to.
The usage of the MyReportLinks.com Books Web site is subject to the terms and conditions stated on the Usage Policy Statement on **www.myreportlinks.com**.
In the future, a password may be required to access the Report Links that back up this book. The password is found on the bottom of page 4 of this book.
Any comments or suggestions can be sent by e-mail to comments@myreportlinks.com or to the address on the back cover.

Photo Credits: © Corel Corporation, pp. 1 (background), 3; Courtesy of LBJ Library, pp. 1, 12, 14, 20, 23, 30, 35, 39; Courtesy of MyReportLinks.com Books, p. 4; Courtesy of The American Experience/PBS, p. 38; Courtesy of The American Presidency/National Museum of American History, Smithsonian Institution, pp. 32, 37; Courtesy of The National Portrait Gallery, p. 41; Courtesy of White House Web site, p. 17; Courtesy of Wildflower Center, p. 42; Department of the Interior, p. 25; John Fitzgerald Kennedy Library, pp. 24, 27; National Archives, pp. 33, 36.

Cover Photo: © Corel Corporation; Yoichi R. Okamoto, LBJ Library Collection.

Contents

MyReportLinks.com Books
Great Books, Great Links, Great for Research!

MyReportLinks.com Books present the information you need to learn about your report subject. In addition, they show you where to go on the Internet for more information. The pre-evaluated Report Links that back up this book are kept up to date on **www.myreportlinks.com**. With the purchase of a MyReportLinks.com Books title, you and your library gain access to the Report Links that specifically back up that book. The Report Links save hours of research time and link to dozens—even hundreds—of Web sites, source documents, and photos related to your report topic.

Please see "To Our Readers" on the Copyright page for important information about this book, the MyReportLinks.com Books Web site, and the Report Links that back up this book.

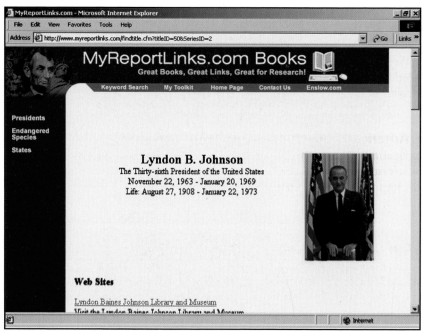

Access:

The Publisher will provide access to the Report Links that back up this book and will try to keep these Report Links up to date on our Web site for three years from the book's first publication date. Please enter **PJH1461** if asked for a password.

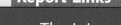
Report Links

➤ The Internet sites described below can be accessed at
http://www.myreportlinks.com

*EDITOR'S CHOICE

▶**Lyndon Baines Johnson Library and Museum**
The Lyndon Baines Johnson Library and Museum contains a wealth of
information about LBJ, including his diary, photographs, presidential
papers, and telephone conversations. You can also take a virtual tour
of the LBJ Museum.

Link to this Internet site from http://www.myreportlinks.com

*EDITOR'S CHOICE

▶**Lady Bird Johnson**
This PBS site provides an inside look at the relationship between Lady
Bird Johnson and Lyndon B. Johnson. Here you will learn how they
met and how she contributed to his success as a politician.

Link to this Internet site from http://www.myreportlinks.com

*EDITOR'S CHOICE

▶**Lyndon B. Johnson: The War on Poverty President**
This site provides a comprehensive biography of Lyndon B. Johnson
where you will learn about his life before, during, and after his
presidency. You also learn about LBJ's foreign and domestic affairs,
his impact on the nation, and his legacy.

Link to this Internet site from http://www.myreportlinks.com

*EDITOR'S CHOICE

▶**The American Experience: Lyndon B. Johnson**
By navigating through this Web site you will find links to Lyndon B.
Johnson's early career, presidential politics, domestic policy, foreign
affairs, legacy, and days of decision.

Link to this Internet site from http://www.myreportlinks.com

*EDITOR'S CHOICE

▶**Lyndon Baines Johnson**
At this site you will find facts and figures on Lyndon B. Johnson,
including links to presidential election results, cabinet members,
historical documents, and other Internet resources.

Link to this Internet site from http://www.myreportlinks.com

*EDITOR'S CHOICE

▶**American Presidents: Lyndon B. Johnson**
At this Web site you will find "Life Facts" and "Did you know trivia?"
about Lyndon B. Johnson. You will also find a letter written by
Lyndon B. Johnson to Lady Bird Taylor, his future wife.

Link to this Internet site from http://www.myreportlinks.com

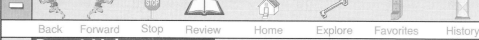

Report Links

The Internet sites described below can be accessed at
http://www.myreportlinks.com

▶**The American Presidency: Hubert H. Humphrey**
At this Web site you will find a brief biography of Lyndon B. Johnson's vice president, Hubert H. Humphrey. Here you will learn about his career in politics and accomplishments as vice president.

Link to this Internet site from http://www.myreportlinks.com

▶**The American Presidency: Lyndon B. Johnson**
This site contains a biography about Lyndon B. Johnson where you will learn about his boyhood, public career, and rise to the presidency. You will also find links to quick facts about LBJ and his inaugural address.

Link to this Internet site from http://www.myreportlinks.com

▶**"I Do Solemnly Swear..."**
At this Web site you will find an image of Lyndon B. Johnson standing beside Jacqueline Kennedy as he is being sworn in as president of the United States.

Link to this Internet site from http://www.myreportlinks.com

▶**The American President: The Professional Politician**
This PBS site profiles four presidents considered to be "professional politicians." Here you will learn how Johnson's handling of the Vietnam War overshadowed the humanitarian progress he made during his administration. You will also find an original document and an audio clip.

Link to this Internet site from http://www.myreportlinks.com

▶**LBJ for Kids!**
This Web site, designed specifically for kids, provides an overview of Lyndon B. Johnson's administration. Here you will learn about Johnson's policies regarding civil rights, the war on poverty, education, the environment, and foreign policy.

Link to this Internet site from http://www.myreportlinks.com

▶**The Lady Bird Johnson Wildflower Center**
In 1982, the Lady Bird Johnson Wildflower Center was founded. At this site you can explore the flowers and plants of Texas.

Link to this Internet site from http://www.myreportlinks.com

Any comments? Contact us: **comments@myreportlinks.com**

Report Links

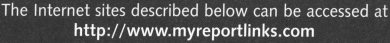

The Internet sites described below can be accessed at
http://www.myreportlinks.com

▶**The Living Room Candidate**
The Living Room Candidate Web site provides campaign footage from
Lyndon B. Johnson's 1964 presidential campaign.

Link to this Internet site from http://www.myreportlinks.com

▶**Lyndon Baines Johnson**
By navigating through this Web site you will find a link to Lyndon
Baines Johnson's biography as well as other biographies of well known
Texans.

Link to this Internet site from http://www.myreportlinks.com

▶**Lyndon Baines Johnson**
Bartleby.com provides a vast collection of electronic documents. Here
you will find Lyndon B. Johnson's inaugural address given on
Wednesday, January 20, 1965.

Link to this Internet site from http://www.myreportlinks.com

▶ **Lyndon B. Johnson**
The National Park Service Web site provides a brief overview of the
Lyndon B. Johnson National Historical Park. You will also find a link
to more detailed information about the park, including Lyndon B.
Johnson's boyhood home and the Johnson Settlement.

Link to this Internet site from http://www.myreportlinks.com

▶**Lyndon B. Johnson**
This site provides an overview of Lyndon B. Johnson's life, early
political career, and presidency. You will also find links to all of
Johnson's State of the Union addresses.

Link to this Internet site from http://www.myreportlinks.com

▶**Lyndon B. Johnson**
The National Portrait Gallery holds a portrait of Lyndon B. Johnson.
There is also a brief profile of LBJ and his administration.

Link to this Internet site from http://www.myreportlinks.com

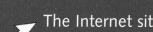

The Internet sites described below can be accessed at
http://www.myreportlinks.com

▶**Lyndon B. Johnson Space Center**
The *Handbook of Texas* Online provides a history of the Lyndon B.
Johnson Space Center. Here you will learn about the accomplishments
of the Johnson Space Center.

Link to this Internet site from http://www.myreportlinks.com

▶**Lyndon B. Johnson (D) vs. Barry M. Goldwater (R)**
The *New York Times* Learning Network provides an overview of the election
of 1964. Here you will also find links to the *New York Times* coverage of the
election and other related articles.

Link to this Internet site from http://www.myreportlinks.com

▶**Man of the Year: Lyndon B. Johnson: The Paradox of Power**
In 1967, Lyndon B. Johnson was again presented with the Man of the Year
award. This article describes how the American people and politicians felt
about Johnson's administration.

Link to this Internet site from http://www.myreportlinks.com

▶**Man of the Year: Lyndon B. Johnson: The Prudent Progressive**
In 1964, Lyndon B. Johnson was presented the Man of the Year award. At
this *Time* magazine Web site you can read the article that evaluates Lyndon B.
Johnson's transition into the office of the presidency.

Link to this Internet site from http://www.myreportlinks.com

▶**Objects from the Presidency**
By navigating through this Web site you will find objects related to all United
States presidents. You will also learn about the era of Johnson's administration
and the office of the presidency.

Link to this Internet site from http://www.myreportlinks.com

▶**President Lyndon B. Johnson**
At this site you will find an interesting fact about LBJ, a quote, a brief
overview of his life, and important events that occurred during his
administration. A list of his cabinet members and Supreme Court
appointees is also included.

Link to this Internet site from http://www.myreportlinks.com

▶**Presidential Transitions "The Torch is Passed"**
At the White House Historical Association Web site you will learn
about John F. Kennedy's assassination and how Lyndon B. Johnson
had to calm an unsettled nation.

Link to this Internet site from http://www.myreportlinks.com

▶**Ruby Shoots Oswald!**
On November 24, 1963, Jack Ruby shot and killed Lee Harvey
Oswald. This Web site contains a letter written by Jack Ruby
and discusses the formation of the Warren Commission under
Lyndon B. Johnson.

Link to this Internet site from http://www.myreportlinks.com

▶**The White House: Claudia Taylor (Lady Bird) Johnson**
The official White House Web site holds the biography of Lady Bird
Johnson. Here you learn about her life and contributions to the Great
Society.

Link to this Internet site from http://www.myreportlinks.com

▶**The White House: Lyndon B. Johnson**
The official White House Web site holds the biography of Lyndon B.
Johnson. Here you will learn about his Great Society program and the
Vietnam crisis.

Link to this Internet site from http://www.myreportlinks.com

▶**Vietnam Online**
Vietnam Online provides a comprehensive overview of the Vietnam
War. Here you will find links to time lines, the key players, reflections
on the war, weapons used, maps, and other references.

Link to this Internet site from http://www.myreportlinks.com

▶**Vietnam War**
At this site you will find a brief overview of the Vietnam War. Here
you will learn about the origins of the conflict and the United States
involvement.

Link to this Internet site from http://www.myreportlinks.com

1908—*Aug. 27:* Lyndon Baines Johnson is born in a three-room farmhouse between Stonewall and Johnson City, Texas.

1918—Follows his father, Sam Ealy Johnson, Jr., on his campaign trail for reelection to the United States House of Representatives.

1926—Joins the Disciple of Christ Church in Texas.

1927—Attends Southwest Texas State Teacher's College.

1928—Crashes the 1928 Houston Democratic Convention with some friends. Directs Welly Hopkins's successful state senate campaign.

1934—*Nov. 17:* Marries Claudia Alta Taylor, known as "Lady Bird." Studies law at Georgetown University.

1935—Becomes director of National Youth Administration in Texas.

1937—Elected to the United States House of Representatives.

1949—Elected to the United States Senate.

1960—Elected as John F. Kennedy's vice president.

1963—*Nov. 22, 2:40 P.M.:* Administered presidential oath in Dallas upon the assassination of President Kennedy.

1964—*May:* Introduces his Great Society in a University of Michigan commencement address.

   —*Aug.:* Johnson calls for Gulf of Tonkin Resolution, unofficially declaring the Vietnam War.

   —*Nov. 3:* Elected president. Declares "War on Poverty" in State of the Union address.

1965—*Jan. 20:* Inaugurated president. The Voting Rights Act of 1965 passes, outlawing discriminatory literacy tests. It causes a considerable increase in minority voting. Medicare and Medicaid established.

1969—*Jan. 20:* Retires to the LBJ Ranch in Texas.

1973—*Jan. 22:* Dies of a heart attack at age sixty-five.

Chapter 1

Tragic Moment, November 23, 1963

Vice President Lyndon B. Johnson could not have asked for a more perfect day. It was a bright and sunny day in Dallas, Texas, on Friday, November 22, 1963. Johnson was riding in a motorcade, with President John F. Kennedy in the lead car, an open convertible. The cavalcade was making its way through the streets of Dallas.

Kennedy and Johnson, a native of Texas, were in Texas as part of a campaign trip. The day before, Kennedy had dedicated four new buildings at the USAF School of Aerospace Medicine at Brooks Air Force Base and had dinner in Houston.

That morning the two had breakfast in Fort Worth. Johnson and Kennedy were scheduled to be in Dallas for a luncheon at noon.

Large groups of people lined the streets as the motorcade moved along. At 12:30 P.M., gun shots rang out suddenly. Vice President Johnson, who was riding in a car a short distance behind President Kennedy's, heard the shots but had no idea where they were coming from.[1]

Instantly, the Secret Service agent assigned to Johnson threw the vice president to the floor of the car. He flung himself on top of the vice president to shield him from any bullets. At that moment, Johnson realized that something was terribly wrong.[2]

With the Secret Service agent on top of Johnson protecting the vice president, the motorcade picked up speed. Johnson's car followed the president's at high speed to Parkland Hospital, a local hospital in the Dallas area.

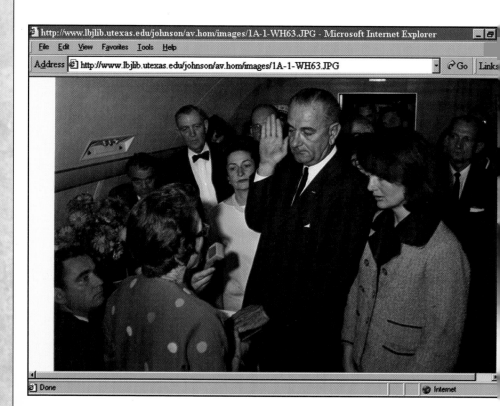

Lyndon Johnson taking the oath of office aboard Air Force One. *Lady Bird Johnson is to his right and Jacqueline Kennedy is to his left. Judge Sarah T. Hughes is administering the oath.*

President Kennedy had been struck in the head and neck by rifle bullets fired by an assassin, believed to be Lee Harvey Oswald. In just a matter of minutes after their arrival, the president was pronounced dead.

At 2:40 P.M., less than two hours after the assassination of Kennedy, the fifty-five-year-old Johnson was sworn in as the thirty-sixth president of the United States. It marked the first time in United States history that a president had been sworn in aboard *Air Force One,* the official presidential airplane.

With Johnson's wife, Claudia Taylor "Lady Bird" Johnson, and Kennedy's widow, Jacqueline, looking on, the oath of office was administered by Federal District Court Judge Sarah T. Hughes. This also marked the first time that a woman had ever sworn in a president.[3]

Just a few minutes later, the jet was airborne. A few hours later, with millions of Americans watching on television, *Air Force One* landed in Washington, D.C. As the casket carrying the body of Kennedy was unloaded from the plane, Johnson made his way to a microphone at the airport.

With Mrs. Johnson at his side, the new president addressed the American public. "I will do my best," said Johnson. "That is all I can do. I ask for your help, and God's."[4]

On November 25, 1963, millions of television viewers from around the world watched as Kennedy was buried at Arlington National Cemetery in Washington, D.C. Just two days later, President Johnson spoke at a joint session of Congress. He spoke of the need to carry out the late president's program:

> All I have I would have given gladly not to be standing here today. . . The greatest leader of our time has been struck down by the foulest deed of our time. Today John Fitzgerald Kennedy lives on in the immortal words and works that he left behind. He lives on in the mind and memories of mankind. He lives on in the hearts of his countrymen. . . No words are sad enough to express our sense of loss. No words are strong enough to express our determination to continue the forward thrust of America that he began.[5]

It was quite a mission for Johnson to help carry out. Johnson came from bleak beginnings, growing up in his hometown of Stonewall, Texas. As a result, there was nothing that was considered too great a challenge for him.

Chapter 2

Early Life, 1908–1935

Lyndon Baines Johnson was born on a ranch in the barren hill country near Stonewall, Texas, on August 27, 1908. He was the eldest of five children, two boys and three girls, born to Samuel and Rebekah Johnson.

Both sides of Johnson's family were pioneers. Both of his grandfathers had been members of the Texas legislature.

▲ Lyndon B. Johnson as a baby.

His father was a farmer and schoolteacher, who also served in the Texas legislature. Johnson's mother was also a schoolteacher, as well as a newspaper editor. So it came as no surprise that young Lyndon learned how to read before he started school.

When Johnson was five, the family moved to Johnson City, Texas, a city that his paternal grandfather, Samuel Ealy Johnson, Sr., had founded. It was about fifteen miles east of Stonewall. Johnson's boyhood home in Johnson City, a one-story frame house, became a National Historic Landmark in 1966.

Like most families in small towns, the Johnsons barely had enough money to live on. If young Lyndon wanted to go to the movies or take part in other types of entertainment, he earned extra spending money by shining shoes and picking cotton.[1]

Young Lyndon attended public school in Johnson City. Although Lyndon was not fond of studying, his mother made sure he did his lessons. For his efforts, Johnson received good grades.

Johnson and Politics

As young Lyndon went through school, he became interested in politics. In high school, he demonstrated a talent for public speaking. He and a friend even won a county-wide debate competition.[2]

A popular boy in school, Lyndon was president of his class of seven students. In 1924, Johnson graduated from high school at the age of fifteen.

Although Johnson's parents wanted him to go to college, Lyndon was tired of school. He was determined to make his own way in the world with no further education.

Crossing the Country

In July 1924, Lyndon and five of his friends set out for California. To earn their way, the group lived the life of hobos. They would pick oranges and wash dishes for meals. They found out just how hard it was to earn money during the farm depression at that time.[3]

Following nearly a year on the road, Johnson hitchhiked back to Johnson City. Instead of going to school, Johnson went to work on a road gang. Although it was hard manual labor, Johnson stuck to the job, despite the urging by both parents to go to college.

College Days

Finally, at eighteen, following a year of road gang work, young Johnson had a change of heart. He borrowed seventy-five dollars from the Johnson City Bank and enrolled in Southwest Texas State Teachers College in San Marcos, Texas.[4]

As he had in his adventure to California, Johnson earned his way through college. He worked as a janitor and then as a secretary for the college president. One year he dropped out of college to earn some extra money. He went to a tiny school in the town of Cotulla, Texas, to teach Mexican-American children. During that experience, Johnson was inspired to help the poverty-stricken students. A desire to help the disadvantaged would stay with him throughout his political career.[5]

Despite missing a year of college, Johnson managed to graduate in 1930 with a degree in history by the time he was twenty-one. It was while he was in college that Johnson tasted his first success in politics. He had organized a campus group called the White Stars. That

Tools   Search   Notes   Discuss   Go!

group took control of campus politics from a group called the Black Stars.[6]

Entering Politics

Following a year of teaching in a Houston high school, an opportunity in politics came along. In 1931, Richard M. Kleberg, a Democrat and owner of the famous King cattle ranch, ran for the U.S. House of Representatives.

When Kleberg won the election, one of the first things he did was to make the twenty-three-year-old Johnson his private secretary and take him along to Washington, D.C. From 1932 to 1935—the last years of the Herbert Hoover

Biography of Lady Bird Johnson - Microsoft Internet Explorer

File   Edit   View   Favorites   Tools   Help

Address http://www.whitehouse.gov/history/firstladies/cj36.html   Go   Links

President   News & Policies   Vice President   History & Tours   First Lady   Search
Oval Office   West Wing   VP Office   Blue Room   East Wing   Library

the White House
President George W. Bush

Your Government   Kids Only   Español   Contact   Privacy Policy   Site Map

Home

Blue Room
Connections

Tours
Tour in Person
Tour On-Line
Botty's Tour

& History
Eisenhower
Executive Office
Building
Facts
First Ladies
Historical
Association
India's Quiz
Presidential
Libraries
Presidents

West Wing
Connections
Policies in Focus
America Responds
Terrorism

Home > History & Tours > Past First Ladies > Claudia Taylor Johnson

Claudia Taylor (Lady Bird) Johnson

Lived: 1912-

Mrs. Lyndon B. Johnson,

Christened Claudia Alta Taylor when she was born in a country mansion near Karnack, Texas, she received her nickname "Lady Bird" as a small child; and as Lady Bird she is known and loved throughout America today. Perhaps that name was prophetic, as there has seldom been a First Lady so attuned to nature and the importance of conserving the environment.

Her mother, Minnie Pattillo Taylor, died when Lady Bird was five, so she was reared by her father, her aunt, and family servants. From her father, Thomas Jefferson Taylor, who had prospered, she learned much about the business world. An excellent student, she also learned to love classical literature. At the University of Texas she earned a bachelor's degree in arts and in journalism.

In 1934 Lady Bird met Lyndon Baines Johnson, then a Congressional

Done   Internet

▲ Claudia Taylor Johnson, nicknamed Lady Bird, was one of the few first ladies to recognize the importance of conserving the environment.

administration and the first years of the Franklin D. Roosevelt administration—Johnson learned how Congress worked.

Lady Bird Meets LBJ

Lyndon B. Johnson met a twenty-one-year-old woman in 1934 during a trip home to Texas. Her name was Claudia Alta Taylor, better known by her nickname, Lady Bird, given to her as an infant by her nurse. Following a whirlwind courtship, twenty-six-year-old Johnson asked Lady Bird to marry him. She accepted, and on November 17, 1934, just two months after they were introduced, the two were married.

Interestingly, Lyndon and Lady Bird had the same initials, LBJ. The Johnsons would eventually have two daughters with the same initials, Lynda Bird and Luci Baines.

The NYA

Fascinated by Franklin D. Roosevelt and his ideas, Johnson idolized the new U.S. president. When President Roosevelt established the National Youth Administration (NYA) in 1935 as a program to help unemployed young people earn money or go to school, Johnson applied for a job with the new organization.[7]

President Roosevelt appointed Johnson the NYA director for Texas. At twenty-six, Johnson was the youngest of the state directors. Through his efforts, about twelve thousand youths went to work on such projects as playgrounds, roadside parks, and soil conservation. With the NYA, Johnson helped thousands of young Americans get through high school or college.[8]

The NYA was just the stepping stone Johnson needed to get his political career off the ground.

Chapter 3 ▶

Career in Politics, 1937–1960

When Congressman James P. Buchanan from Johnson's Tenth Congressional district in Texas died, a special election was called to fill the vacancy. Not surprisingly, Johnson decided to run for the position.

Johnson was running against nine other candidates. Out of the ten candidates, Johnson was the only one who strongly supported the policies of President Franklin D. Roosevelt and his New Deal.[1] Johnson used that as his political platform as he campaigned throughout his district. In the end, Johnson won the election on April 17, 1937, receiving three thousand more votes than the nearest candidate.

▶ Roosevelt and Johnson

Following Johnson's victory, Roosevelt, who was vacationing off the Texas coast at the time, invited the twenty-eight-year-old congressman to visit him. Johnson accepted and developed a personal friendship with the president.

In later years, Johnson would describe Roosevelt as being "like a daddy to me."[2] Johnson also developed another strong relationship in Washington with Sam Rayburn. Rayburn, the majority leader of the House of Representatives, had once been a fellow state legislator with Johnson's father in Texas. Johnson learned valuable lessons from both Rayburn and Roosevelt.

Thanks to his relationship with Roosevelt, Johnson had direct access to the White House. That would later help him

▲ Lyndon and Lady Bird Johnson at the LBJ Ranch.

secure choice committee assignments and gain federal projects for his district. One was a program that provided cheap electricity for farmers under the new Rural Electrification Administration (REA).

Johnson also sponsored projects that gave his home district help with soil conservation, public housing, lower railroad freight rates, and expanded credit for loans to farmers. He did such a good job for his Texas congressional district that he ran unopposed for reelection in 1938, 1940, and 1942.

Johnson Runs for Senate

In April 1941, Morris Sheppard, the senior U.S. senator from Texas, died. Immediately, Johnson ran as a candidate to fill the remainder of the term. Despite his strong campaign efforts and over 600,000 votes cast, Johnson lost to conservative Texas Governor W. Lee O'Daniel by a narrow margin of 1,311 votes.[3] Johnson returned to Washington and his duties in the House of Representatives.

World War II

On December 7, 1941, the Japanese bombed the U.S. Naval Base in Pearl Harbor, Hawaii. Johnson, who had been a member of the Naval Reserve for several years, asked to be called to active duty. Johnson's answer came on December 11, when he was sworn in as a lieutenant commander. He became the first member of the House of Representatives to go into uniform.

Johnson was sent to the South Pacific as a special representative of the president. He participated as an observer on a bombing mission. During the mission, the plane in which he was flying was shot by Japanese fighter planes. For his efforts, Johnson was presented with the Silver Star for gallantry under enemy fire.

Then, in July 1942, President Roosevelt ordered that all members of Congress, including Johnson, be placed on inactive duty and return to their legislative posts in Washington.

Lady Bird in Business

It was during the 1940s that Mrs. Johnson, a sound businesswoman, began purchasing radio, and later, television stations in Texas. The Johnsons eventually acquired the three hundred-acre LBJ Ranch, thirteen miles west of Johnson City, as well as an 1,800-acre ranch nearby.[4]

Johnson Runs Again for Senate

By 1948, thirty-nine-year-old Johnson was again ready to run for a U.S. Senate seat. He was one of eleven candidates to enter the Democratic primary.

Using a helicopter, something that many Texans had not seen, Johnson crisscrossed the state campaigning. When the July vote came, Johnson, with 405,617 votes, finished second to Governor Coke Stevenson, who had 477,077.[5]

A run-off election was held to determine the true winner. With approximately one million votes cast, Johnson won by just eighty-seven votes. He was nicknamed Landslide Lyndon as a joke. Although there were allegations of voter fraud on both sides, and a lawsuit by Stevenson contesting the result, Johnson was declared the winner, and became a U.S. senator.

Just like he did in Congress, Johnson immediately jumped into his Senate duties and soon became highly regarded by the Senate leadership. Johnson was appointed to the Senate Armed Services Committee in 1950. He became increasingly concerned with the country's military readiness during the Cold War with the Soviet Union.

Johnson also became chairman of the Preparedness Investigating Subcommittee. During the Korean War, Johnson's committee saved the United States more than an estimated $5 billion and strengthened the armed forces.

▶ Influential Senator

By 1951, Johnson had become a force in the Senate. That same year, the Democratic senators elected Johnson as deputy majority leader, or "whip," of the Senate. While serving in this capacity, Johnson strengthened his ability to persuade men to reach agreement.

When the Democrats lost control of the Senate following the 1952 elections, Johnson was unanimously selected as minority leader. At forty-four, Johnson was the youngest man either party had ever chosen as a Senate leader.

Johnson was reelected to the Senate in 1954, this time winning by 70 percent of the vote. Because there were now more Democrats than Republicans in the Senate, Johnson became majority leader of the Senate in January 1955. By this time, he was becoming known for his ability to put together a majority vote for his side on almost any issue.

Unfortunately, Johnson suffered a severe heart attack on July 2, 1955. The strain of eighteen-hour days had finally caught up with the Texas senator. Although he returned to the Senate in January 1956, Johnson's health was a cause for concern for the rest of his life.

Many believe Johnson's greatest moment as a majority leader came with the passage of the Civil Rights Acts of 1957 and 1960. The 1957 bill was the first civil rights act since the Reconstruction period following the Civil War. The 1960 bill was passed despite a filibuster by some senators from the South. A filibuster is an attempt by senators to stall long enough so that a vote on bill will not take place. The acts were designed to help black Americans achieve equal voting rights with white Americans.

Johnson also became a strong supporter of the exploration of outer space. He became the first chairman of the Senate Aeronautical and Space Committee. Johnson sponsored the law that helped establish the National Aeronautics and Space Administration (NASA).

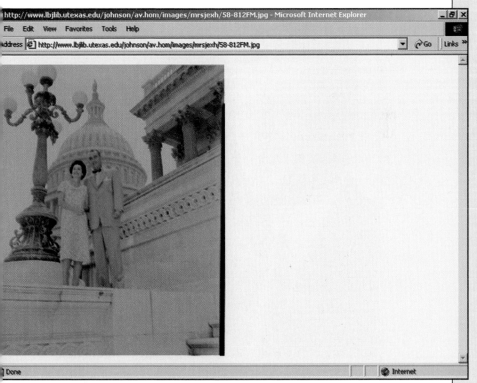

▲ *Senator and Mrs. Johnson at the Capitol building in 1958.*

Chapter 4

Vice President, 1960–1963

As powerful and successful as Lyndon Johnson had been as a congressman and senator, there was never a doubt in anyone's mind who knew him that he wanted to become president. That is why it came as no surprise when Johnson announced his candidacy for the Democratic presidential

▲ *John F. Kennedy and Lyndon B. Johnson during the 1960 presidential campaign.*

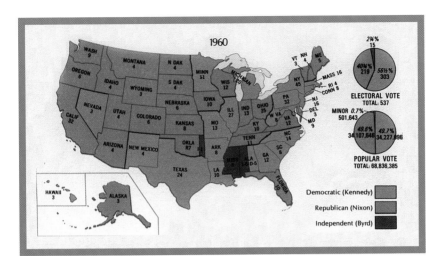

▲ *This map shows the results of the presidential election of 1960.*

nomination a week before the party's July 1960 national convention in Los Angeles, California.

Unfortunately for Johnson, Senator John F. Kennedy of Massachusetts had the nomination sewn up. On the first ballot at the convention, Senator Kennedy received 806 votes to Senator Johnson's 409. Only 761 were needed, so Kennedy was nominated.

▶ Johnson for Vice President

Then, in a surprise move, Kennedy asked Johnson if he would like to run for vice president. Kennedy believed that with Johnson on the ticket, the duo would be able to carry most of the South, which Johnson represented, and win the election.

"And I am grateful, finally, that I can rely in the coming months on so many others—on a distinguished running-mate who brings unity to our ticket and strength to our Platform, Lyndon Johnson." said Kennedy at the convention.[1]

Johnson accepted the nomination and immediately hit the campaign trail as hard as he ever had in his life. After three months of campaigning, it was time for the people to decide. In the November election, Kennedy and Johnson narrowly defeated the Republican team of Vice President Richard M. Nixon and Senator Henry Cabot Lodge of Massachusetts. It was the electoral votes from the southern states of Texas, Louisiana, New Mexico, and Nevada that carried the Democratic duo.

Interestingly, Johnson was also reelected to his third six-year term as Texas senator at the same time.

▶ Johnson Busy as Vice President

Upon taking the oath of office as vice president in January 1961, Johnson resigned from the Senate. In typical Johnson fashion, the new vice president took a more active role in the government than any previous vice president ever had.

Johnson served as chairman of the National Aeronautics and Space Council, the President's Committee on Equal Employment Opportunity, and the Peace Corps National Advisory Council.

The Texas native was also sent by the president on many foreign missions, especially to world trouble spots during the Cold War, as Kennedy's representative. In August 1961, Johnson was sent to the divided nation of Germany. With the Berlin Wall dividing West and East Berlin, Johnson reassured West Berliners that the United States was standing firmly behind them.[2]

Johnson also traveled to other parts of Europe, Africa, South Asia, the Far East, the Middle East, and Latin America.

During his first few years as vice president, Johnson dealt with many sensitive issues, such as the Cuban Missile Crisis in 1962. This photo shows where some of the Soviet missiles in Cuba were located.

Fatal Trip to Texas

In late 1963, Johnson joined President Kennedy on a trip to Texas. Many looked at the trip as being an early investment for the upcoming 1964 Kennedy–Johnson campaign.[3] It had been generally felt that Kennedy had once again lost support in Texas, which carried many electoral votes.

The trip began on November 21, with stops in Houston and San Antonio. Surprisingly large and somewhat friendly crowds turned out to greet the president and vice president.

The political duo moved on to Forth Worth and Dallas on November 22. The day began with a breakfast presentation in Fort Worth in the morning. They continued to Dallas for a mid-day appearance. It was at the same site where Johnson had nearly been assaulted only three years earlier.[4]

Again, as in the other three cities they had appeared in, the crowds seemed quite friendly. As part of their appearance in Dallas, an open convertible carried Kennedy and Texas Governor John Connally. Johnson rode in another car two car lengths behind Kennedy's.

At about 12:30 P.M., as the lead car carrying Kennedy turned the corner in front of the Texas Schoolbook Depository, a number of shots rang out.

Although Johnson did not know it at the time, soon after the bullets entered Kennedy's skull, the vice president inherited the duties of president of the United States. A half hour later, doctors declared JFK dead. Governor Connally had also been shot, but survived and recovered.

At 2:40 P.M. on *Air Force One*, with the body of the late president on board, Johnson was sworn in as president by Judge Sarah T. Hughes. Lyndon Baines Johnson was now the thirty-sixth president of the United States.

Chapter 5 ▶

President Johnson, 1963–1966

It only took Lyndon B. Johnson three minutes after taking over as president to give his first order: "Now, let's get airborne."[1] *Air Force One* took off from Dallas, and flew back to Washington, D.C., carrying the nation's new president, along with the body of the late President Kennedy.

Following the funeral of Kennedy on Monday, November 25, the mournful United States, now led by Johnson, moved ahead. LBJ moved quickly to win congressional approval for legislation proposed by the Kennedy administration that had not yet passed.

▶ Johnson Moves Ahead

In his first State of the Union address given to Congress on January 8, 1964, Johnson stated his intent to fulfill many of Kennedy's programs:

> Let this session of Congress be known as the session which did more for civil rights than the last hundred sessions combined; as the session which enacted the most far-reaching tax cut of our time; as the session which declared all-out war on human poverty and unemployment in these United States; as the session which reformed our tangled transportation and transit policies; as the session which achieved the most effective, efficient foreign aid program ever; and as the session which helped to build more homes and more schools and more libraries and more hospitals than any single session of Congress in the history of our Republic.[2]

The passing of the Civil Rights Act of 1964, the Economic Act establishing the antipoverty program, and a tax reduction bill designed to stimulate the economy, were the major accomplishments of Johnson's first year in office.

In a speech given by Johnson in May 1964, he stated that ". . . we have the opportunity to move not only toward the rich society, but upward to the Great Society."[3]

▶ Johnson's Great Society

It did not take long for the term "Great Society" to catch on with the American public. It would eventually be used to describe many of the president's domestic programs.

http://www.lbjlib.utexas.edu/johnson/av.hom/images/276-10-64.JPG - Microsoft Internet Explorer

File Edit View Favorites Tools Help

Address http://www.lbjlib.utexas.edu/johnson/av.hom/images/276-10-64.JPG   Go   Link

Done   Internet

▲ Johnson signing the Civil Rights Act of 1964. Over the president's left shoulder are Martin Luther King, Jr., and Barry Goldwater.

By July 1964, the Republican National Convention had named Senator Barry Goldwater of Arizona as its candidate for president. Goldwater had voted against the Civil Rights Act of 1964. His vice-presidential running mate was Congressman William E. Miller of New York.

Johnson Nominated for President

The Democratic National Convention met in August and easily nominated Johnson as their choice for president. Minutes after his nomination, which occurred on his birthday, Johnson asked that Senator Hubert H. Humphrey of Minnesota be nominated as the Democratic choice for vice president. He was approved without opposition.

In the November elections, the Johnson–Humphrey ticket won by one of the largest landslides in American history. They received 61.1 percent of the popular vote.[4] They received 486 electoral votes to only 52 for the Goldwater–Miller ticket. The victorious duo also carried 44 of the 50 states and the District of Columbia.

Johnson's victory, in part, stemmed from his assurances that he would not expand the nation's role in Southeast Asia.[5] Yet he was not the first president to send troops there. Dwight D. Eisenhower was the first president to send military advisers to Vietnam to aid the South Vietnamese government. President Kennedy had increased greatly the number of United States military advisers to sixteen thousand.

Johnson's assurances that he would not escalate the war came despite an incident that had occurred back on August 2, 1964, that would ignite the longest war in United States history.[6] On that day, the American destroyer *Maddox*, patrolling in the Gulf of Tonkin off the

coast of North Vietnam, was attacked by three torpedo boats. They did little damage and were driven away.

Then, a second attack was supposed to have taken place two nights later against the *Maddox* and her sister ship, the U.S.S. *Turner Joy.* The only evidence of attack came from some mysterious blips on a radar screen. These attacks became known as the Gulf of Tonkin Incident.

▶ United States Enters Vietnam War

Although uncertain reports put some doubt on the episode, President Johnson ordered retaliatory air strikes "against gunboats and certain supporting facilities" in North Vietnam.[7]

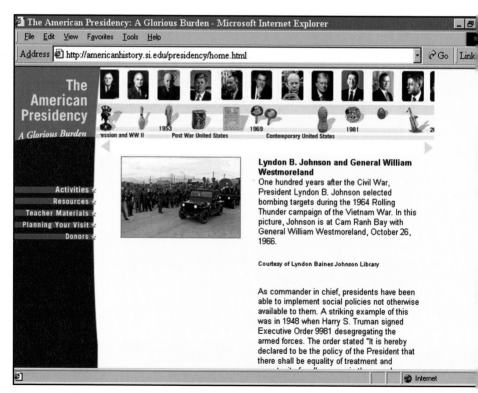

The American Presidency: A Glorious Burden - Microsoft Internet Explorer

File   Edit   View   Favorites   Tools   Help

Address 🗐 http://americanhistory.si.edu/presidency/home.html   ⟳ Go   Link

The American Presidency
A Glorious Burden

1953   Post War United States   1969   Contemporary United States   1981

Activities
Resources
Teacher Materials
Planning Your Visit
Donors

Lyndon B. Johnson and General William Westmoreland
One hundred years after the Civil War, President Lyndon B. Johnson selected bombing targets during the 1964 Rolling Thunder campaign of the Vietnam War. In this picture, Johnson is at Cam Ranh Bay with General William Westmoreland, October 26, 1966.

Courtesy of Lyndon Baines Johnson Library

As commander in chief, presidents have been able to implement social policies not otherwise available to them. A striking example of this was in 1948 when Harry S. Truman signed Executive Order 9981 desegregating the armed forces. The order stated "It is hereby declared to be the policy of the President that there shall be equality of treatment and

🌐 Internet

▲ *Johnson is pictured here with General William Westmoreland at Cam Ranh Bay in October 1966.*

▲ Many school segregation protests were held during Johnson's administration, despite his attempts to establish equal human rights among American citizens.

Johnson then asked Congress for approval of a resolution "to promote the maintenance of international peace and security in Southeast Asia."[8] The vote came almost unanimously from both the House and Senate. The Gulf of Tonkin Resolution was passed.

By 1965, United States citizens began to discover the reality of a war in Vietnam as it continued to grow. From 23,000 military advisers stationed in Vietnam in 1964, U.S. troop strength grew to 184,000 in 1965.[9] Johnson

then sent an additional 200,000 troops to Vietnam in 1966. By 1968, American forces in Southeast Asia were at more than 500,000. By that time, American battle deaths had reached over thirty thousand.

▶ Johnson Faces Problems Back Home

Back home in the United States, Johnson continued his attempts at tackling the problem of racism. Early in 1965, Johnson spoke before a joint session of Congress and an audience of millions of television viewers on the topic of race relations.

> The command of the Constitution is plain. There is no moral issue. It is wrong—deadly wrong—to deny any of your fellow Americans the right to vote in this country.
>
> There is no states' rights or national rights. There is only the struggle for human rights . . . It is the effort of American Negroes to secure for themselves the full blessings of American life. Their cause must be our cause too. Because it is not just Negroes, but really it is all of us who must overcome the crippling legacy of bigotry and injustice. And . . . we . . . shall . . . overcome."[10]

Following a brief moment of stunned silence, the chamber exploded with applause. Congressmen, senators, and the gallery alike all stood and cheered, with some even crying. It turned out to be the president's finest hour. The speech became one of the most famous in American political history.

Johnson continued to promote his Great Society, attempting along the way to have Congress pass some wide-ranging programs. Many Great Society proposals were passed by Congress between 1965 and 1967. Among them were those providing protection of voting rights, medical care for the aged (Medicare), federal aid for education,

▲ *Johnson is pictured here signing the Medicare Bill in 1965, with former president Truman seated next to him. Standing over Johnson's left shoulder from left to right are Lady Bird Johnson, Vice President Humphrey, and Elizabeth Truman.*

immigration reform, and an increased minimum wage. Two new cabinet-level departments, Housing and Urban Development (1965) and Transportation (1966) were created.[11]

Unfortunately for Johnson, he faced several problems. The expanding war in Vietnam was unpopular with many Americans. There was also an unhappiness with the ideals of the Great Society and a backlash against the Johnson administration's civil rights program. In addition, many lawmakers felt the Vietnam War and Johnson's Great Society programs were costing too much money. Those all hurt the Democratic Party in the 1966 elections. Although the Democrats still controlled the Senate and Congress, their majorities were not as great.

▲ By 1966, Johnson's popularity had dropped considerably due to the growing anti-Vietnam War sentiments. In this photo, protesters square off with military police. The woman is offering the soldier a flower as a symbol of gentleness and love.

▶ Johnson Unpopular

LBJ's popularity had dropped drastically by 1966. There was a growing antiwar sentiment. The Vietnam War had seriously divided the United States. Many opposed the war and demonstrated to prove their point. In 1965 for example, thousands of people supported the war. Still, many Americans protested at the White House. Soon, President Johnson would have the most difficult time of his political career.

Johnson's Later Days, 1967–1973

Between 1966 and 1967, violence in the United States continued to grow. Part of it was a result of protests against the war in Vietnam. Another part of it came from the poor African Americans living in some of the nation's larger cities. They were dissatisfied with how they were treated in society, and believed that funds they should be receiving were going to the war effort.

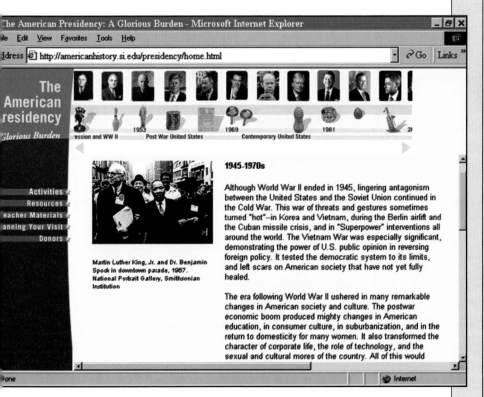

▲ Martin Luther King, Jr., in a downtown parade in 1967.

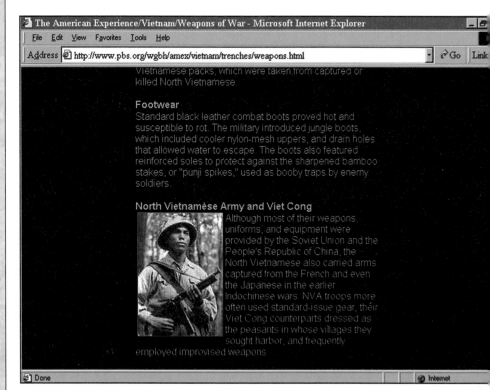

The American Experience/Vietnam/Weapons of War - Microsoft Internet Explorer

File   Edit   View   Favorites   Tools   Help

Address http://www.pbs.org/wgbh/amex/vietnam/trenches/weapons.html   Go   Link

Vietnamese packs, which were taken from captured or killed North Vietnamese.

Footwear
Standard black leather combat boots proved hot and susceptible to rot. The military introduced jungle boots, which included cooler nylon-mesh uppers, and drain holes that allowed water to escape. The boots also featured reinforced soles to protect against the sharpened bamboo stakes, or "punji spikes," used as booby traps by enemy soldiers.

North Vietnamese Army and Viet Cong
Although most of their weapons, uniforms, and equipment were provided by the Soviet Union and the People's Republic of China, the North Vietnamese also carried arms captured from the French and even the Japanese in the earlier Indochinese wars. NVA troops more often used standard-issue gear, their Viet Cong counterparts dressed as the peasants in whose villages they sought harbor, and frequently employed improvised weapons.

Done   Internet

▲ *North Vietnamese soldiers were supported by the Soviet Union and China. Aside from uniformed soldiers, U.S. troops also had to contend with the Viet Cong. The Viet Cong dressed in regular clothes, but would carry out attacks on American and South Vietnamese troops.*

This is what Lyndon B. Johnson faced each day during the latter part of his presidential term. Riots broke out in many cities' African-American ghettos during those two years. When civil rights leader Reverend Martin Luther King, Jr., was killed on April 4, 1968, in Memphis, Tennessee, riots exploded in over one hundred cities across the United States. Johnson even had to call out federal troops to calm down the rioting taking place in his own backyard of Washington, D.C. On the positive side, Thurgood Marshall became the first African American on the Supreme Court.

Tough Year for LBJ

The year 1968 is considered to be one of the most agonizing years in United States history.[1] Not only did Johnson have to face the problems of the Vietnam War, but on January 8, 1968, it was reported that North Korea had seized the United States Navy intelligence ship U.S.S. *Pueblo*. In that situation, LBJ used diplomacy rather than retaliation.

"I do not want to win the argument and lose the sale," explained Johnson.[2] Diplomacy worked when the *Pueblo* crew was released at the end of the year.

Still, the war in Vietnam was an ongoing problem. The low point for Americans came during Tet, the Vietnamese holiday that celebrates the lunar new year. Viet Cong and North Vietnamese forces, attacking at night, launched an all-out attack against cities and military posts in South Vietnam. South Vietnamese cities fell. Several American air bases were shelled.

While President Johnson believed that the Tet offensive had failed because the enemy had lost almost 45,000 men, he admitted that it had been a victory in their minds. Any hope of the war ending soon were gone with this outburst.

Another election year arrived. In the New Hampshire primary held in March 1968, Senator Eugene McCarthy of Minnesota had won almost as many votes as LBJ. Following that primary, New Yorker Robert F.

Attorney General ▶
Robert Kennedy.

Kennedy, brother of the late President John F. Kennedy, announced his candidacy for the Democratic presidential nomination. On the day Robert F. Kennedy said he was running, a public opinion poll was taken that showed that Johnson's popularity had dropped to a new low.[3]

During this time, LBJ had repeatedly sent messages to North Vietnam, asking for negotiations to end the fighting. The messages were rejected. Instead, the North Vietnamese asked that the United States end its bombing of North Vietnam and remove its military from South Vietnam.

As the war raged on, Johnson continued sending troops over to Vietnam. The more he sent, the worse things got.[4]

▶ LBJ Makes a Decision

On March 31, 1968, President Johnson went on television and made a surprising move. Addressing the nation, Johnson stated that he was going to reverse United States actions and lessen the bombings on North Vietnam. He hoped that by limiting the bombing, peace talks might begin. Then the president made an even more startling announcement.

"There is a division in the American house...I have concluded that I should not permit the presidency to become involved in the partisan divisions that are developing in this political year . . . Accordingly, I shall not seek, and I will not accept, the nomination of my party for another term as your president."[5] Ironically, peace talks began in Paris the following month.

The only high note for Johnson in 1968 occurred on December 24, when United States astronauts orbited the moon for the first time in history. The NASA space program, which Johnson had supported over the years, gave the president one final, shining moment in his political career.

Johnson's Final Years

Johnson left office in 1969 and retired to the LBJ Ranch. While there, he wrote his memoirs in 1971, *The Vantage Point: Perspectives of the Presidency, 1963–1969*. That same year he also helped to plan the Lyndon Baines Johnson Library in Austin, Texas.

It was also during this time that Johnson's health began to fail. On January 22, 1973, one day before President

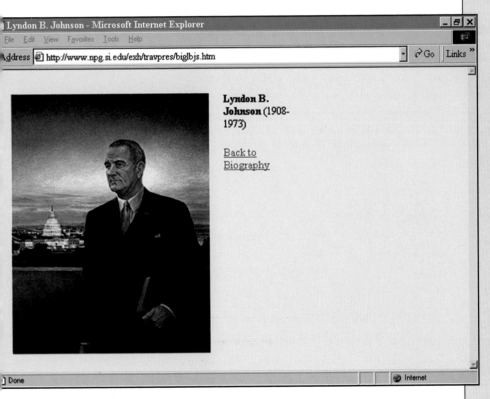

Lyndon B. Johnson - Microsoft Internet Explorer

File   Edit   View   Favorites   Tools   Help

Address http://www.npg.si.edu/exh/travpres/biglbjs.htm   Go   Links

Lyndon B. Johnson (1908-1973)

Back to Biography

Done   Internet

Although he was thrust unexpectedly into the presidency, Johnson did his best to raise social and civil rights awareness in the United States.

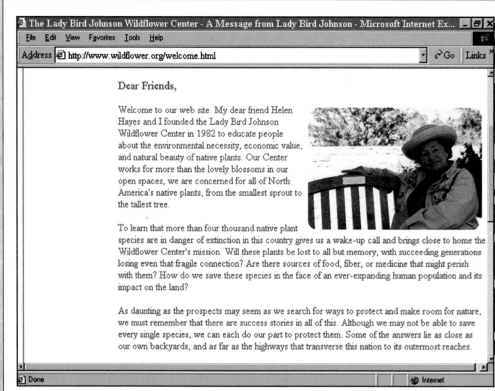

Dear Friends,

Welcome to our web site. My dear friend Helen Hayes and I founded the Lady Bird Johnson Wildflower Center in 1982 to educate people about the environmental necessity, economic value, and natural beauty of native plants. Our Center works for more than the lovely blossoms in our open spaces, we are concerned for all of North America's native plants, from the smallest sprout to the tallest tree.

To learn that more than four thousand native plant species are in danger of extinction in this country gives us a wake-up call and brings close to home the Wildflower Center's mission. Will these plants be lost to all but memory, with succeeding generations losing even that fragile connection? Are there sources of food, fiber, or medicine that might perish with them? How do we save these species in the face of an ever-expanding human population and its impact on the land?

As daunting as the prospects may seem as we search for ways to protect and make room for nature, we must remember that there are success stories in all of this. Although we may not be able to save every single species, we can each do our part to protect them. Some of the answers lie as close as our own backyards, and as far as the highways that transverse this nation to its outermost reaches.

▲ Lady Bird Johnson founded the Wildflower Center in 1982. The organization is designed to educate people about the environment and the necessity of native plants.

Richard M. Nixon announced a cease-fire agreement with Vietnam, Lyndon Baines Johnson died of a heart attack at the age of sixty-four.

It was revealed that several days before Johnson's death, Nixon had informed LBJ by phone of the approaching peace agreement.

Johnson's body was flown to Washington, D.C., for memorial services. It was flown in the same plane in which he had been sworn in as president nine years earlier. Following the memorial services, LBJ's body was flown back to Texas. He was buried in a family graveyard, beside his parents and grandparents on the banks of Pedernales River.

▶ Johnson Remembered

Johnson's presidency ended in frustration and with the country divided. It came as no surprise that after Johnson left office he avoided active participation in any political activities.

Following Johnson's death in 1973, the Manned Spacecraft Center in Houston, Texas was renamed the Lyndon B. Johnson Space Center. The Texas state legislature later passed legislation that made August 27, Johnson's birthday, a legal holiday in the state.

When Johnson left the presidency in 1969, he was not one of the more popular presidents of his time, especially because of the Vietnam War. The war would continue on several more years past Johnson's death. Unfortunately, Johnson's name and the Vietnam War will forever be thought of as one.

Interestingly enough, a 2000 survey of seventy-eight scholars by the Federalist Society and the *Wall Street Journal* showed that Johnson is now considered to be an above average president. The scholars ranked thirty-nine of the presidents, from George Washington to Bill Clinton. Johnson was ranked No. 17, just behind James Monroe and ahead of John F. Kennedy.

Chapter 1. Tragic Moment, November 23, 1963

1. David C. Whitney, *The American Presidents* (New York: Doubleday & Company, Inc., 1985), p. 321.

2. Ibid.

3. Ibid.

4. Lyndon B. Johnson, Oath of Office speech, November 23, 1963, reprinted online, "The Presidency: 'The Government Still Lives,'" *The Kennedys*, 1999, <http://www.time.com/time/daily/special/kennedy/8.html> (February 11, 2002).

5. Lyndon B. Johnson, address before a joint session of Congress, November 27, 1963.

Chapter 2. Early Life, 1908–1935

1. David C. Whitney, *The American Presidents* (New York: Doubleday & Company, Inc., 1985), p. 316.

2. William A. DeGregorio, *The Complete Book of U.S. Presidents* (New York: Dembner Books, 1984), p. 565.

3. Whitney, p. 316.

4. Ibid.

5. Robert Dallek, "Lyndon B. Johnson," *Character Above All: Essays*, n.d., <http://www.pbs.org/newshour/character/essays/johnson.html> (February 11, 2002).

6. DeGregorio, p. 565.

7. *The Presidents Collection—LBJ*, PBS Home Video, Turner Home Entertainment, Inc., 1997, videocassette.

8. DeGregorio, p. 567.

Chapter 3. Career in Politics, 1937–1960

1. David C. Whitney, *The American Presidents* (New York: Doubleday & Company, Inc., 1985), p. 317.

2. *The Presidents Collection—LBJ*, PBS Home Video, Turner Home Entertainment, Inc., 1997, videocassette.

3. Whitney, p. 317.

4. *The Presidents Collection—LBJ*, videocassette.

5. Whitney, p. 318.

Chapter 4. Vice President, 1960–1963

1. John F. Kennedy, "Democratic National Convention Acceptance Speech," reprinted online at *John F. Kennedy Memorial Page*, n.d., <http://www.jfkin61.com/photo _speech/convention.html> (February 11, 2002).

2. *The Presidents Collection—LBJ*, PBS Home Video, Turner Home Entertainment, Inc., 1997, videocassette.

3. Paul K. Conkin, *Big Daddy From The Pedernales: Lyndon Baines Johnson* (Boston: Twayne Publishers, 1986), p. 170.

4. Ibid.

Chapter 5. President Johnson, 1963–1966

1. Merriman Smith, "Eyewitness: The Death of President Kennedy, November 22, 1963," *Merriman Smith's Eyewitness Account*, n.d., <http://www.auburn.edu/ ~lowrygr/kennedy.html> (February 11, 2002).

2. Lyndon B. Johnson, "Annual Message to the Congress of the State of the Union, January 8, 1964," reprinted online at *The Lyndon B. Johnson Library and Museum,* n.d., <www.lbjlib.utexas.edu/johnson/archives.hom/speeches.hom /640108.asp> (February 11, 2002).

3. Lyndon B. Johnson, "The Great Society," published on line at *Speeches by Lyndon B. Johnson,* n.d., <http://www .tamu.edu/scom/pres/speeches/lbgreat.html> (February 11, 2002).

4. David C. Whitney, *The American Presidents* (New York: Doubleday & Company, Inc., 1985), p. 322.

5. *The Presidents Collection—LBJ*, videocassette.

6. Paul Halsall, ed., "The Tonkin Bay Resolution, 1964," *Modern History Sourcebook, 1998,* <http://www.fordham.edu/halsall/mod/1964Tonkinbay.html> (February 11, 2002).

7. Joseph Newman, ed., *200 Years—A Bicentennial Illustrated History of the United States, 1776–1976* (D.C.: U.S. News & World Report, Inc., 1973), p. 269.

8. Ibid.

9. Ibid.

10. Lyndon B. Johnson, "We Shall Overcome," reprinted online at *Education India,* 2000-2002 Cyber Initiatives, Ltd, <http://www.stanfordplus.com/education/inspirationals/johnsonovercome.php> (February 11, 2002).

11. *The Presidents Collection—LBJ,* videocassette.

Chapter 6. Johnson's Later Days, 1967–1973

1. Joseph Newman, ed., *200 Years—A Bicentennial Illustrated History of the United States, 1776–1976* (D.C.: U.S. News & World Report, Inc., 1973), p. 273.

2. Ibid.

3. Ibid.

4. *The Presidents Collection—LBJ,* PBS Home Video, Turner Home Entertainment, Inc., 1997, videocassette.

5. Newman, p. 273.

Further Reading

Becker, Elizabeth. *America's Vietnam War: A Narrative History*. New York: Houghton Mifflin Company, 1992.

Collins, David and Melissa Roberts, ed. *The Long Legged School Teacher: Lyndon Baines Johnson, from the Texas Hill Country to the White House*. Austin, Tex.: Eakin Press, 1987.

Denenberg, Barry. *Voices from Vietnam*. New York: Scholastic, Inc., 1995.

Eskow, Dennis. *Lyndon Baines Johnson*. Danbury, Conn.: Franklin Watts, Inc., 1993.

Falkof, Lucille and Richard G. Young, ed. *Lyndon B. Johnson: Thirty-Sixth President of the United States*. Ada, Okla.: Garrett Education Corporation, 1989.

Gay, Kathlyn and Martin K. Gay. *Vietnam War*. Brookfield, Conn.: Twenty-First Century Books, Inc., 1996.

Hunt, Michael H. *Lyndon Johnson's War: America's Cold War Crusade in Vietnam, 1945–1968*. New York: Hill & Wang, 1997.

Joseph, Paul. *Lyndon B. Johnson*. Edina, Minn.: ABDO Publishing Company, 2000.

Lindop, Edmund. *Dwight D. Eisenhower, John F. Kennedy, Lyndon B. Johnson*. Brookfield, Conn.: Twenty-First Century Books, Inc., 1996.

Marrin, Albert. *America & Vietnam: The Elephant & the Tiger*. New York: Penguin Putnam Books for Young Readers, 1992.

Schuman, Michael. *Lyndon B. Johnson*. Springfield, N.J.: Enslow Publishers, Inc., 1998.

Schwab, Orrin. *Defending the Free World: John F. Kennedy, Lyndon Johnson & the Vietnam War, 1961–1965*. Westport, Conn.: Greenwood Publishing Group, Inc., 1998.

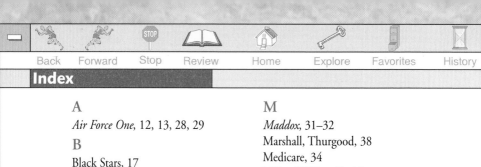